THE OVER-THE-HILL SURVIVAL GUIDE

How to keep young people in their place, get back at your kids, and go out with a bang

Bob Feigel
and
Malcolm Walker

Meadowbrook Press
Distributed by Simon & Schuster
New York

Library of Congress Cataloging-in-Publication Data

Feigel, Bob [Senior citizen's survival guide] The over-the-hill survival guide:
        how to keep young people in their place, get back at your kids,
        and go out with a bang/Bob Feigel and Malcolm Walker.
        P.   cm.
         1. Aged—Life skill guides—Humor.   I. Walker, Malcolm, 1950-
II. Title.
PN6231.A43F45   1989   818'.5402—dc20   89-33822
ISBN:0-88166-169-4

Editor: Bruce Lansky
Production Editor: Sandy McCullough
Art Director: Cathy Cullinane-Skraba
Production Manager: Pam Scheunemann
Cover and interior design: Michael Smith

Simon & Schuster Ordering #:0-671-69000-0

Published by Meadowbrook Press, 18318 Minnetonka Boulevard,
Deephaven, MN 55391.
BOOK TRADE DISTRIBUTION by Simon & Schuster, a division of Simon and
Schuster, Inc., 1230 Avenue of the Americas, New York, NY 10020.

First published in 1988 under the title *The Senior Citizen's Survival Guide* by
SeTo Publishing, Auckland, New Zealand.

89 90 91 92 5 4 3 2 1

Printed in the United States of America.

CONTENTS

INTRODUCTION

THE SENIOR CITIZEN

In enlightened societies, Senior Citizens are venerated. They are placed high upon pedestals of honor and respect. They are listened to by their children and their children's children. Their opinions are cherished as priceless pearls of wisdom. Senior Citizens are treasured in their Golden Years. Pampered through the autumn of their lives. Best of all, their wishes are carried out before they are! In enlightened societies, the older you get, the better life gets. Too bad your friends and family don't understand.

A RAW DEAL

So, what's it like being a Senior Citizen in western society? Bleak. Just think, you've spent a lifetime working, paying taxes, playing by the rules...and now, just when your investment should start paying dividends, you're dumped. Retired from your job. Exiled to geriatric ghettos for the gray. Suddenly no one is listening. Years of experience mean nothing. Your opinions don't count. You've been sentenced to an almost ghost-like existence on the sidelines of society. No doubt about it—you're getting a raw deal.

FIGHTING BACK

Then why not retaliate? Get even? Fight back and change this rotten, superficial, youth-oriented culture and transform it into an enlightened society where age is respected, not ridiculed. This little handbook was written to help you survive the indignities of old age and turn the tables on the young upstarts who, in the immortal words of Rodney Dangerfield, "don't give you no respect."

Turn the tables on the young upstarts who "don't give you no respect."

SHOPLIFTING FOR BEGINNERS

In view of today's economy, shoplifting should be thought of as a self-help program designed to give Senior Citizens a practical alternative to starvation. But there are rules....

Look upon shoplifting as an adventure, and remember Robin Hood.

BASIC RULES

DON'T FEEL GUILTY

If you're going to feel guilty, you might as well skip this section and go straight to Creative Cooking with Pet Foods. (See page 10.)

DON'T BE GREEDY

Be selective. Use this practical survival skill to supplement basics like bread and water with prohibitively expensive luxuries like meat, cheese, butter, coffee, soap, and laxatives.

DON'T BE OBVIOUS

Try not to draw attention to yourself. Better still, work in pairs and get an accomplice to create a timely diversion while you hobble into action. Like any other professional skill, shoplifting requires patience and practice. So if at first you don't succeed, try, try, try again.

Don't be greedy.

Shoplifting the wrong way.

Shoplifting the right way.

THE CHILD IN THE BABY CARRIAGE TRICK

Borrow a child who's still young enough to babble incoherently. Borrow a baby carriage to put it in. If you can get paid for baby-sitting at the same time, so much the better!

Grab one of those hand-held shopping baskets on the way into the supermarket and fill it with unwanted basics while stuffing expensive luxury items underneath the child.

As you approach the checkout counter, casually lean down to the child and firmly pinch one of its pudgy little thighs. Use a hat pin if you prefer.

Appear concerned but helpless as the child erupts into a fit of megadecibel rage that drives everyone around you bonkers.

Should the child show any sign of calming down, pinch, tweak, or stick it again and again so that it is screaming bloody murder by the time you reach the checkout counter.

Apologize profusely to the cashier, dump your basket of basics on the counter, and head quickly for the nearest exit.

Everyone will be so delighted to see both of you go that no one will think to search the baby carriage.

Appear concerned but helpless.

CREATIVE COOKING WITH PET FOODS

You have probably noticed that pet foods are really catching on with Senior Citizens these days.

Why?

Why not! Pet foods are packed with protein, nutritionally balanced, and a great source of fiber. They are convenient, versatile, and easy to use.

So why waste them on pets?

Why waste pet food on pets?

YOU ARE WHAT YOU EAT

Poverty aside, pet foods have become nutritionally superior to most people foods. Compare the label on a can of dog food with the label on a can of beef stew. You'll be surprised.

DEHYDRATED LEFTOVER VEGETABLES, NON-FAT MILK SOLIDS, VARIOUS SPICES, ASSORTED FLAVORINGS, CULINARY EXTRACTS, STABILIZERS, PRESERVATIVES, THICKENERS, COLORING, ACID REGULATORS EMULSIFIERS, ANTICOAGULANTS ANTIREGURGITATORS NONSPECIFIED MEAT CHUNKS BITS, PIECES, STUFF, THINGS, SUGAR, SALT, MSG.

Chef WALDO ®
HAUTE·CUISINE·IN·A·CAN
ANOTHER FINE PRODUCT FROM CHEF WALDO INTERNATIONALE
·CAIRO·CALCUTTA·MANILA·
·PORT-AU-PRINCE·WAGGA WAGGA·

WOOF WOOF
☙ DOG FOOD ☙
· INGREDIENTS ·
SELECTED FILET MIGNON TRIMMINGS, PRIME BEEF BY-PRODUCTS ORGANICALLY GROWN VEGETABLES BIODYNAMIC CEREALS, FRESH WHEY PROTEIN, NATURAL GELLING AGENTS, POLYUNSATURATED VEGETABLE OIL, SPECIAL FLAVOURINGS IMPORTED SPICES, & T.L.C (TENDER LOVING CARE) ALSO WITH ADDED PHOSPHOROUS POTASSIUM, MAGNESIUM, ZINC IRON, VITAMINS, RIBOFLAVIN NIACIN, YOU NAME IT, ITS GOT IT. CALORIES PER KG · 1200
NOT FOR HUMAN CONSUMPTION

Which would you rather eat?

MEMORABLE MEALS

Combine your favorite recipes with a variety of pet foods for a series of memorable meals in a jiffy. Replace outrageously expensive meat and fish with wholesome, value-packed pet foods today!

OUR CHEF SUGGESTS:

BREAKFASTS
Purina Porridge
Gaines Granola
Scrambled Eggs and Snausages

LIGHT LUNCHES
Chuckwagon Chili
Liv-a-snaps Paté
Ken-L-Ration Croquettes
Kit 'N Kaboodle Quiche

HEARTY MAINS
Meaty Bone Stew
Gravy Train Goulash
Mighty Dog Meat Loaf
Alpo à la King

SUCCULENT SEAFOODS
Butcher's Blend Bisque
Nine Lives Newburg

ETHNIC DELIGHTS
Mexican: Tender Vittles Tacos
English: King Kuts Wellington
Cajun: Kibbles Creole
French: Vets *Au Vin*
Japanese: Tuffy's Teriyaki
Italian: Crave Cacciatore
Chinese: Kal Kan Cantonese

DELICIOUS DESSERTS
Meow Mix Milk Shake
Pounce Pudding
Seed Cake à la Mode

SAMPLE RECIPE

MIGHTY DOG MEAT LOAF

The beauty of cooking with pet foods is that most of the ingredients are already included.

Here's all you need for this moist meat loaf:

3 large cans of Mighty Dog dog food
1 large onion
1 tbsp. cooking oil
a deep, loaf-shaped, "nonstick" baking pan

1. Empty contents of Mighty Dog cans into large mixing bowl.
2. Gently sauté onion in oil.
3. Mix sautéed onion with Mighty Dog in mixing bowl.
4. Dump everything into the baking pan.
5. Place in oven on medium heat for 10 minutes.

Serves 4 adults or 1 teenager.

Gently sauté to perfection.

ENTERTAINING FOR THE IMPOVERISHED

If the high cost of entertaining is all that's keeping you from throwing a gala dinner party then have a look at this:

Aperitif—"Atilla" after-shave (you can find countless unused bottles of this uniquely aromatic fluid at the local garbage dump shortly after Father's Day).

Main Course—Assorted vegetables freshly selected from your grocer's trash and Ruff Natural Dog Food (shoplifted).

House Wine—Raspberry Kool-Aid in methylated spirits (shoplifted).

Dessert—Ten milligram tabs of Valium suspended in lime Jell-O and eaten with chopsticks.

Note: Should you desire a meatier main course, get in the habit of setting traps for small animals or neighborhood pets.

Don't let the high cost of entertaining keep you from throwing a party.

GLAMOUR HINTS FOR GERIATRICS

Growing old feels bad enough without having to look the part as well. But thanks to modern cosmetic surgery, you can fold back the years, tuck away the ravages of time, and look young again. At least, from the neck up!

DO-IT-YOURSELF FACE-LIFTS

Unfortunately, cosmetic surgery has become so expensive that Senior Citizens are resorting to do-it-yourself face-lifting. Despite obvious drawbacks, all you need are some helping hands, a firm grip, and a little imagination.

STAYING IN STYLE

Just because you are old and impoverished doesn't mean you can't dress in style. Maybe not this year's style. Maybe not even last year's style. But at least some year's style! So check out your local secondhand clothing shop. After all, the clothes you gave away to charity twenty years ago just might be this season's haute couture.

Always take care to ensure that your old body can keep up with your new face.

SELF-DEFENSE

Being a Senior Citizen these days is worse than being on the Endangered Species list. Not only do you stand a good chance of being mugged, burglarized, or having your purse snatched, you're fair game for every human parasite from con artists to tax collectors. Sad to say, today's society dismisses Senior Citizens as an obsolete minority group not worth protecting. Worse, they see you as a hopeless group of decaying old has-beens on automatic self-destruct. (For more insulting terms, see the list on page 60.)

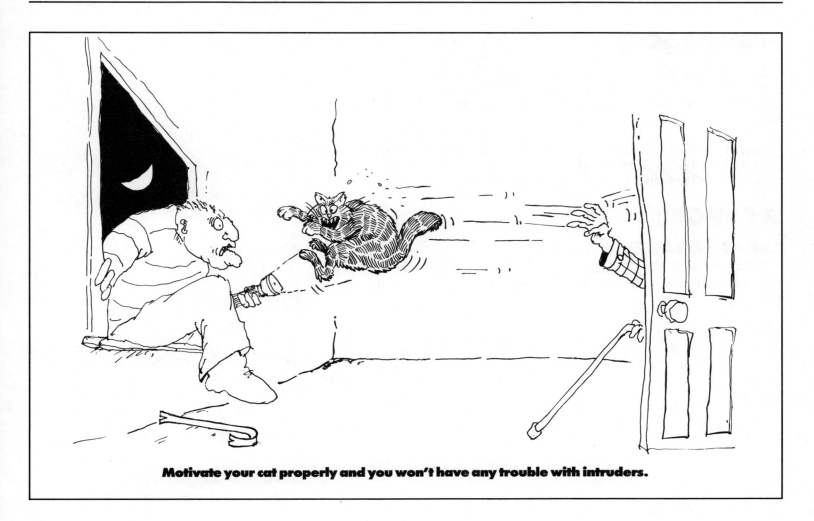

Motivate your cat properly and you won't have any trouble with intruders.

FIGHT BACK!

So what if you're a bit rusty and worn-out. So what if you can't fight with your fists. You're still a long way from being that doddering, moth-eaten old fossil they think you are. (For even more insulting terms, try the same list.)

Even if you can't outrun 'em, you can outsmart 'em. Besides, who would expect a helpless, crumbling old relic like you to use sophisticated self-defense techniques like these?

WEAPONS

CANES AND SWORD STICKS

The trouble with these traditional weapons is that bludgeoning takes up too much energy and punctured arteries are so messy.

Unfortunately, bludgeoning burglars with your cane takes too much energy.

CAMERA FLASH

A small pocket camera with a built-in flash is perfect to temporarily blind your attacker, thus giving you a chance to introduce your steel-toed walking shoes to the soft parts of his body. This was good enough for Jimmy Stewart in Hitchcock's *Rear Window*, remember?

UMBRELLAS

The metal tips on some models can be sharpened to a lethal point. Firmly shoving an automatic umbrella down an assailant's throat and triggering it can cause extreme discomfort.

Keep the metal tip of your umbrella well sharpened.

BANK BOOKS

Say you're being menaced by some great hulking thug and all you've got to defend yourself with is a bank book. No problem. Simply hold your bank book open in front of his face and let the attacker read it. He'll feel so depressed by your pitiful bank balance that he will press a few coins into your hand and go away.

PILLS

If the odds are stacked against you and you have to run away, this little trick can save your life. Get as far ahead of your pursuer as possible and spill your bottle of pills directly in his path. He'll either slip on them and fall down or he'll give up the chase in fear of catching whatever dread disease you no longer possess medication to combat.

Note: Don't use the last of your heart pills for this!

Spill your vitamins or cough drops directly in the path of your pursuer.

22

DIVERSIONS

PALSY

Faking palsy requires more coordination than acting skill and can be very useful as a delaying tactic in a one-on-one confrontation. First, make sure you carry a sock filled with sand inside your trousers or skirt and a pocketful of loose change. When accosted and asked for money, start shaking and fish out a handful of change. Offer it to your attacker, shaking so hard it falls to the ground at his feet. As your assailant bends down to pick it up, whip out the sock full of sand and put him away.

BLINDNESS

For this scam you'll need mirrored sunglasses, steel-toed footwear, and a white cane weighted with lead. Thinking that you are easy pickings, a mugger will approach you openly as you shuffle and tap your way through the rougher parts of town. Using your cane, "feel" your way toward your mugger and tap around his feet. Stop, do your Stevie Wonder act, and say in a quavering voice, "Is anybody there?" This will appeal to the mugger's perverted sense of humor and give you the chance to kick him in the shins with your steel-toed shoe. While he's hopping around, remember that this trick will only work once, so quickly decide which part of his body to break with your lead-filled cane.

Remember to wear your steel-toed shoes.

TWO WAYS TO MAIM WITH A CRUTCH

Killing with a crutch is easy. It's maiming that takes skill. First, determine if you need crutches to keep upright. If so, use only one at a time or you'll fall down.

Caution: Do not attempt these techniques on stairs, moving escalators, or waxed floors.

THE ONE-CRUTCH CROTCH CRUNCHER

Wait until your assailant is within striking distance, then suddenly look beyond him so that he thinks someone is coming up from behind. As he turns to look, bring your left crutch right up between his legs with enough force to lift him to his toes. This will cause him great pain followed by intense agony. Take advantage of this moment to smash him over the back of the head and limp away quickly.

Give him "The old one...

THE TWO-CRUTCH PINCHER

Judge your assailant's distance. Look him straight in the eye. Aim for the neck. Swing your right crutch, follow through with your left, and pinch until he loses consciousness.

...two."

25

HOME PROTECTION

GRANDCHILDREN

When it comes to laying booby traps, grandchildren are indispensable. Pick a room nearest to the most obvious "burglar" entry point to your home. Buy lots of toys, marbles, roller skates, dolls, etc., and invite your grandchildren or neighbor's children over to play. Throw them out after half an hour; that will be enough. Ask them to be sure and tidy up before they go. Then close up the room and never invite them back. Any burglar entering this room is history.

SPRAY-PAINT CANS

Here is the perfect weapon to use on children. Always shake the can before opening the door or paying a visit to your grandchildren.

FEAR

Instead of a traditional security system that sounds an alarm everyone, including the police, ignores, install one that turns on a tape recorder with this message:

Welcome to the home of Don "Vicious" Vincente, recently retired Godfather of the local Family. The Don is sorry he has missed you, but he is out visiting the surviving relatives of the last person who entered his house without permission. Please do not leave a message, as hidden cameras have already recorded your identity. Have a nice day.

Always shake the can of spray paint before opening the door for your grandchildren.

GROUP TACTICS

Unless you're a confirmed masochist or are contemplating suicide, plan any foray into enemy territory with military precision.

Send out a suitable decoy to lull the enemy into a false sense of security, then spring a trap that will make Custer's Last Stand look like a tea party.

Deploy a suitable decoy.

REVENGE, SWEET REVENGE

Whoever said that revenge isn't fun must have been a Junior Citizen. Besides, you might not get another chance.

ANNOYING YOUR CHILDREN

PAY THEM A VISIT AND...

- Take along all your dirty laundry.
- Go straight to the refrigerator, carefully study the contents with the door open, complain that there's nothing you like, then devour everything in sight.
- Leave a mess in every room, and make sure you turn on all the lights.
- Tie up the telephone for hours, making long distance calls wherever possible.
- Break a few of their favorite glasses.
- Get up earlier than they do and use up all the milk/coffee/tea.
- Switch on the TV then leave the room.
- Crank up the volume on the stereo and insist you're hard of hearing when they ask you to turn it down.
- Become suddenly ill when asked to do anything around the house. Or claim you have to do homework for an adult education course you're taking.
- Come for a week, stay for eight, and pay for nothing.
- Slam the door every time you leave.
- Borrow their car and return it with a near-empty fuel tank.
- Or, borrow their car, come home without it, and say that you can't remember where you left it.

Raid their refrigerator and devour everything in sight.

THE GOLDEN RULES

- Borrow money, tools, clothes, etc., and never return them.
- Call them collect from faraway places and ask them to send you the fare home.
- Forget all their birthdays.
- Phone them early Sunday morning, during dinner, or in the middle of their favorite TV show, and say you feel lonely and just thought you'd have a little chat.
- Encourage your grandchildren to do all the rotten things their parents did at their age.
- Never miss a chance to tell them they just don't understand what it's like to be your age.

Encourage your grandchildren to do what their parents did.

EMBARRASSING THEM

One sure way to embarrass your kids is to dress in your best clothes and turn up at your son or daughter's place of work when you are sure he or she is away. Proudly tell everyone in sight that it's your birthday and you are being taken out to lunch. When someone explains that your offspring isn't there, say "Oh! Seems I've been forgotten again..." and shuffle sadly away. Or try one of these:

■ Surprise them at their pool or hot-tub party by jumping in nude.
■ Pretend to be a vegetarian at their barbecue and harass all their meat-eating guests.
■ Dance at their wedding.
■ Gate-crash their office party and make a pass at the boss or the boss's spouse.
■ Show up at their dinner party dressed in your grubbiest gardening clothes and beg for food.

Surprise them by jumping in nude.

Show up at their dinner party dressed in your grubbiest gardening clothes and beg for food.

WORRYING THEM

If you have second thoughts about worrying your children, simply cast your mind back to those sleepless nights, missed meals, and gray hairs. Here are a few useful phrases to use on them:

- It's not too late to change my will, you know.
- Lately I've been thinking about getting married again.
- We've always counted on spending our last days with you.
- What would you say about me joining one of those communes?
- Let's spend as much money as we can before we die.

And if none of the above work, take off on a two-week vacation and don't tell them.

MAKING THEM FEEL GUILTY

Parents have been making their children feel guilty since the beginning of time, so why stop a good thing now? Here are some more useful phrases:

- You wouldn't talk like that if your father was still alive.
- Your mother would turn in her grave if she heard you.
- How can you say that, after all I've done for you.
- And to think what I've sacrificed for YOU!
- Don't worry about me. You have your own life to live (accompanied by sigh).
- I guess I'm just no good for anything anymore.
- You won't have me to push around much longer.
- I could shrivel up and die for all you care.
- At least my cat loves me.

Tell them you've been thinking of spending your last days with them.

SOME ADVANTAGES OF BEING OLD

Growing old is not as bad as it's cracked up to be. There are some definite advantages that accompany the aches and pains of old age.

ON THE PLUS SIDE

- Meals on Wheels drivers flirt with you.
- Buying a round of drinks down at the corner bar gets cheaper as your friends die off.
- Underwear doesn't have to be changed so often.
- No one tries to sell you life insurance any more.
- Religious nuts don't try as hard to recruit you, although they are still happy to hit you up for donations.

HOW TO GET RID OF OBNOXIOUS RELIGIOUS HUSTLERS

- Ask for a receipt.
- Say you haven't seen their guru/leader since you served time together for fraud and are sorry to see he still hasn't gone straight.
- If they're from an eastern cult, invite them to your next Bible class.
- If they're "Bible Thumpers," invite them to your ashram.
- If they're neither, invite them to your séance.

Tell religious nuts to get lost or you'll report them to the Better Business Bureau.

SENILITY AS A CON

The nicest thing about taking advantage of your age is that you're only doing what young people expect, and therefore deserve.

SHOPPING

DISCOUNT SHOPPING

In the checkout line appear confused as you count out your money, and put down less than required. When the clerk points out your mistake, take all the money back and start again. After a while the clerk will pay the difference just to get rid of you.

FASTER SHOPPING

Senior Citizens should not be expected to spend their Golden Years standing around in supermarkets, waiting to be checked out. Either go straight to the front of the line, butt in, and pretend you're deaf should anyone complain, or push your fully laden shopping cart up to the "10 items or less" counter, ignoring all the dirty looks.

Act confused when counting out your change.

PUBLIC TRANSPORTATION

FREE BUS RIDES

Push to the front of the line, using your cane on shins when necessary. Get on first and stall the driver with small talk and questions while fumbling around your pockets or purse for money.

Continue this routine until the folks behind you start grumbling to the driver, and someone—anyone—offers to pay your fare.

NO STANDING

If all seats are full, limp painfully up to the nearest Junior Citizen, demand his seat, and wheeze directly into his face until he moves. When seated, start telling your life story to the person next to you, and soon you will be able to stretch out in comfort.

EATING OUT

FREE LUNCH

Choose a decent restaurant. Enjoy an expensive meal. Walk out without paying. If someone runs after you demanding payment, insist you've paid...you remember it clearly...or at least you don't remember ever having forgotten before...besides, here's the receipt (here produce a bus ticket)...who put that there?...and so on. Considering what it's costing someone to listen to such drivel, there will eventually come a time when you're left to digest your meal in peace.

Stretch out in comfort when you finally get a seat.

OUT TO PASTURE

In some societies, Senior Citizens are expected to spend the last years of their lives living in the comfort of the family home, surrounded by their children, grandchildren, and great-grandchildren. In others, old people are more or less expected to walk out into the wilderness and die alone. With a choice like that, maybe retirement communities aren't such a bad idea after all.

Most people wish Senior Citizens would go "out to pasture" and stay there until they die.

CHOOSING THE RIGHT SPOT

Whether it's a huge community of several thousand or a smaller, more intimate little retirement village, it is a good idea to check it out carefully before signing on the dotted line. Here are some rules to follow:

- Don't involve your children. They don't have to live there; you do.
- Pretend to be checking the place out for YOUR parents. You'll get an idea of what you can really expect.

Pack a photo of your family. You may never see them again.

WHAT TO LOOK FOR

After your official tour with the manager, insist on a "quiet hour" by yourself to "get a feel for the place." Now's your chance:

- Cross-examine a few inmates.
- Check out the kitchen cupboards for suspicious quantities of pet food.
- Take a sample of the water for analysis. Some places put embalming fluid into the drinking water to keep everyone looking younger.
- If appropriate, invite yourself to the next meal and insist on eating what the residents eat. Compare this to what the residents are paying for it.
- Inspect the records of the local ambulance service. Be wary of an unusually high turnover rate.

Make sure to check the caretaker's arms for strange tattoos. You can never be too careful!

COMBATING BOREDOM

OK. You've chosen your retirement spot and moved in. Now what? Here are some suggestions to make sure that at least you're not bored to death:

- Home brew is not only a fascinating hobby, it can make you many friends. Start out with beer and ale and graduate to your own still. Bathtub gin will ensure your popularity.
- Infiltrate the local Bridge Club and introduce a porn video night.
- Set up a gambling ring that takes bets on who's going to kick the bucket next. (No fair cheating.)
- Invite local Peeping Toms to start a neighborhood watch group.
- Organize practical adult education classes like "Do-It-Yourself Casket Making," "Euthanasia for Beginners," and "How to Con the Welfare Agencies."
- Sabotage the speed controls on the golf carts.

Show porn videos after an exhausting bridge tournament.

THE LAST LAUGH

You may not be able to avoid the inevitable, but with a little forethought, a smidgen of imagination, and a dollop of good old vindictive bile, you can make sure that those you leave behind know damn well "who got the last laugh"!

Arrange for a tour of your favorite whiskey distillery, and at the appropriate moment, "fall" into the vat of your choice—it should not be difficult to avoid rescuers.

Visit the newspaper you like most, wait until the final edition is rolling, then hurl yourself between the press's rollers—you'll make the front page!

Hire a hit man and outsmart him as long as you can.

Tell a gang member how silly he looks.

Dive into a bath of varnish and become the world's largest door stop.

Make an effort to outdo Evel Knievel—get out your old easy-riding machine, head for the Grand Canyon, and let 'er rip.

GOING OUT WITH A BANG

With burial space at a premium these days, more and more people are opting for cremation.

BIG BANG

By the time anyone finds out you've stuffed your do-it-yourself casket with high explosives, you'll be long gone.

CHINESE NEW YEAR

Insist on being decked out in a favorite suit or dress previously lined with firecrackers.

FRESH AIR FAREWELL (or Hire-A-Pyre)

For that al fresco funeral, line up a couple of old army buddies who, at the appropriate moment, will step forward with flame-throwers and really see you out.

Stuff your casket with high explosives.

53

THE LAST WORD

For the last word in burials, have a tape player hidden in your casket. Get a friend to set the remote control to activate your voice just as the casket goes down.

Ask a friend to activate your voice just as the casket descends.

THE BARGAIN BURIAL

Inexpensive burials don't necessarily have to be in cardboard caskets, especially with a little previous planning—and a little help from your friends.

- Have yourself packed and anonymously shipped to the Internal Revenue Service. COD.
- Arrange for a friend to stuff you into a trash bag and put you out on the pavement on garbage day.

Arrange for a friend to stuff you into a trash bag and put you out on the pavement on garbage day.

OVER THE TOP

Cheap funerals might not suit everybody, so here's an expensive but memorable idea.

SHOW TIME

You'll need a Hollywood producer to work closely with an Archbishop on this extravaganza, as nothing less than a large cathedral will do.

After a suitable solemn introduction by his Bishopness, exotically clad dancers from Caesar's Palace, Las Vegas, will perform a choreographed version of your life. This will be followed by a selection of your favorite songs performed by the New York Philharmonic Orchestra under the baton of Bruce Springsteen. The eulogy will be delivered...with appropriate pauses...by Ronald Reagan, reading from a script prepared by Kurt Waldheim's speech writer. Your lead-lined, gold-and-silver-encrusted casket will ride comfortably to your resting place in a custom-built Masserati hearse and be buried with full military honors by surviving members of Anwar Sadat's bodyguard.

Your children will be sent the bill.

Arrange for show girls to dance on your casket.

WHERE THERE'S A WILL...

This is definitely your last chance to hit 'em where it hurts.

A properly attested will is a forever document. It is not only your Last Testament—it is your Last Way To Drive Them Nuts!

Here are a few suggestions:
- leave everything to the Dallas Cowboys Cheerleaders Retirement Fund
- or to the Arnold Schwarzenegger for President Fund
- or to the Ronald Reagan Home for the Self-Embalmed
- or stick a pin into the Beijing telephone directory
- or leave little treasure maps for everyone, with riddles for them to solve before they can find the loot you've hidden away over the years

But don't forget to leave a copy of this book to each of your children. One day they will need it too.

A WILL WITH A TWIST

Now that you've been laid to rest, you might as well have one more last laugh.

To ensure a large gathering of family, friends, business associates, neighbors, etc., have your lawyer invite everyone you've ever known to a large hall for the reading of your will—suggesting they might learn "something to their advantage."

When they are all quietly seated, have your lawyer invite each guest to get up and say a few nice words about you. Each will be given a copy of a video you recorded before your passing, which your lawyer will then play on a large screen set up for the purpose. This is your last chance to say all the things you've ever wanted to say to various individuals in the audience. Recommend that they enjoy the party afterward because all of your money went to pay for it.

Videotape your final message...you'll have a captive audience.

INSULTING TERMS

ancient old heap
at death's door
bag of bones
bumbling old twit
cantankerous old coot
crumbling
crusty old fart
decayed old fart
dingbat
doddering old twit
dotard
dusty
falling apart at the
    seams
fuddy-duddy
gone to seed
gray-haired
had it

has-been
ineffectual old twerp
infirm
living on borrowed time
long-in-the-tooth
museum piece
moldy oldy
no spring chicken
moth-eaten
obsolete
oldy but moldy
old-timer
old fogey
old fool
old fussbudget
one foot in the grave
ornery old cuss
ossified old fossil

out of the Ark
over the hill
passé
past it
past your prime
rickety old geezer
ruin
rusty
shriveled
silly old dingbat
stale
stubborn old goat
tiresome old geek
toothless relic
way past it
worm fodder
worn-out
wrinkles